King Leonard's Celebration

Written by Christopher A. Lane
Illustrated by Sharon Dahl

A Sonflower Book

VICTOR BOOKS®

A DIVISION OF SCRIPTURE PRESS PUBLICATIONS INC.
USA CANADA ENGLAND

Dedicated
to the King above all kings.
May Your kingdom come.

KIDDERMINSTER KINGDOM TALES
King Leonard's Celebration
Sir Humphrey's Honeystands
Nicholas and His Neighbors
Cornelius T. Mouse and Sons

1 2 3 4 5 6 7 8 9 10 Printing/Year 94 93 92 91 90

ISBN: 0-89693-846-8

VICTOR BOOKS
A division of SP Publications, Inc.
Wheaton, Illinois 60187

King Leonard's Celebration

There was a lion king who ruled over all the beasts of the Kingdom of Kidderminster. His name was Leonard, and he lived in a majestic castle high atop a mountain in the center of a jungle. He seldom ventured down from his beautiful palace, but instead watched over his subjects by gazing out over the kingdom through his royal telescope.

Leonard was a very kind king and greatly enjoyed doing good things for his subjects. He thought it quite delightful to give the animals gifts and presents in secret. Sometimes he would have his servants leave bushels of bananas or baskets of figs on the doorsteps of their jungle homes, or would dispatch the royal gardeners to plant rare flowers in their yards.

King Leonard also loved to protect the animals. If a large hungry animal ventured into the jungle, King Leonard himself would go down and frighten it away with a mighty roar.

But the other animals never saw him. In fact, some thought that he was only a fairy tale. Others had heard stories of his sharp claws and huge teeth and thought he was a fierce, cruel lion. The rest of the animals didn't much care. They just kept all of his wonderful gifts and presents and went about their merry way.

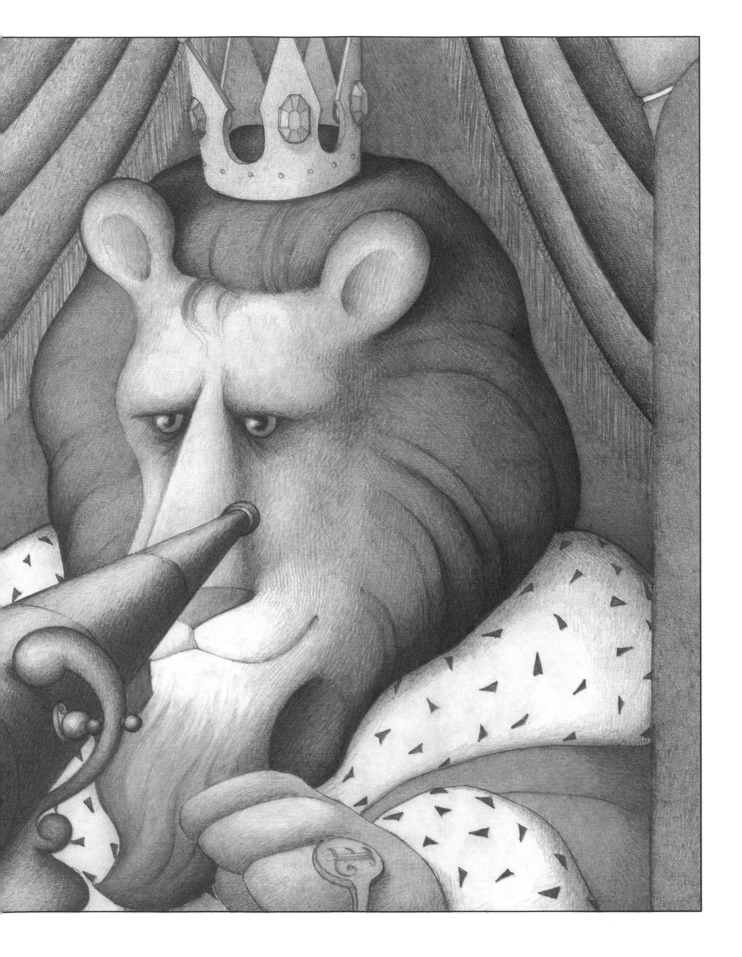

One fine summer day as King Leonard sat upon his throne, he had an idea.

"Horatio!" the king bellowed, nearly losing his crown.

A few moments later a tall, thin bird clothed in a colorful kingdom uniform scurried up to the throne.

"You called, Sire?" he asked.

"Yes, Horatio," King Leonard began. "I have had a wonderful idea. I would like to do something for my jungle subjects."

"But, Sire," Horatio objected, "you gave them a fresh supply of bananas and figs only yesterday."

"Yes, yes, I know that," the king said. "But I would like to do something . . . something special for them."

"What more could you do, Sire?" Horatio asked. "You've already given them enough cause to celebrate."

"That's it, a celebration!" the royal lion shouted, grabbing the bird with his large paws. "You've hit upon it, Horatio! We shall have an extra special celebration!"

"Sire?" the bird asked.

"I shall give my subjects a party. There shall be fine foods, games, balloons, cakes, music, noisemakers, puzzles, and . . . ice cream. Yes! Prepare gallons and gallons of ice cream in the royal ballroom. Oh, this will be so much fun."

"Where would you like to hold this 'celebration,' Sire?" Horatio asked. "In the jungle streets or by the stream perhaps?"

"No, no, don't be silly, Horatio," King Leonard chuckled. "I will invite all the animals here to my palace."

"But, Sire," the bird objected, "all of them? And they have never—"

"Yes, yes, I know," the king nodded, "they have never been here before. Well, it is high time they came. Now, we will have the party tomorrow. Begin the preparations immediately."

So a royal decree was issued and the king's fleet-footed messengers ran to and fro, leaving invitations in the mailboxes of all the jungle animals.

The next morning, King Leonard was busy preparing for the big event. He had his servants assist him into his most special robe. He ordered for his crown to be polished to a lustrous sheen.

Meanwhile, the king's fleet-footed messengers went to and fro throughout the kingdom asking the animals if they would be attending the royal celebration.

One messenger went to Henry Hyena's home. Knocking at the door, he could hear someone inside laughing very loudly. After some time, the hyena finally answered the door.

"What do you want?" Henry asked with a chuckle.

"Mr. Hyena," the messenger explained, "I have been sent to inquire about whether or not you will be coming to King Leonard's celebration today."

"King Leonard?" Henry smirked. "That's a good one."

"Sir," the messenger tried again, "the king has requested your presence at—"

"King schming," Henry joked, "don't gimme that hooey! You don't expect me to believe there really is a King Leonard, do you?"

"Then I take it you will not be attending his party this afternoon?" the messenger asked.

"You don't give up, do you?" Henry laughed. "Ah, I'd really like to," he jested, "but I, ah, I just bought the Sahara Desert and thought I'd go take a look at it. Get it? Do you get it? I bought the Sahara . . ."

Before the royal messenger could explain to the laughing hyena that there really was a king and that there really was to be a celebration, Henry slammed the door in his face.

At the house of Zelda the Zebra, another messenger was knocking at the door. His arrival had already been announced by the barking of Ms. Zebra's two energetic dogs. He waited patiently as Zelda peered out at him through the window and then eyed him through the peephole in the door.

"Down, Somba! Down, Simba!" Zelda said forcefully. "Who is it?" she asked, still not opening the door.

"A royal messenger, Ma'am," the servant shouted.

"What do you want?"

"I have come to ask if you will be attending King Leonard's celebration."

"Are you telling me that that mean lion is having a party?" Zelda asked. "Oh, no, you don't. You can't fool me that easily."

"Excuse me, Ma'am," the messenger continued, "King Leonard has invited you to a celebration this afternoon. There will be plenty of food and —"

"Oh, sure," Zelda answered, "and I'm the main course, right?"

"Oh, no, no," the messenger explained, "King Leonard is truly very kind. Now, I really must know if you are planning to attend."

"I doubt it," Zelda said sternly. "I just bought a pair of watch dogs and, boy, are they fierce. I'll be busy teaching them to attack intruders this afternoon."

"Well, then, good day, Ma'am," the messenger said, marking out Ms. Zebra's name.

Another messenger approached the house of Marvin Monkey and pulled a long vine to ring his doorbell.

"Can you get the door, Sugar?" one voice shouted.

"Sure thing, Honeybunch," another voice responded.

Suddenly the door opened and out swung Marvin Monkey.

"Good morning, Mr. Monkey," the messenger said brightly. "I have come to ask if you plan to attend King Leonard's celebration this afternoon."

"Celebration?" Marvin asked.

"Yes, you should have received an invitation," the messenger explained.

"Oh, yeah, that thing," Marvin said, scratching his head. "We ain't comin'."

"I beg your pardon?"

"We ain't comin'," Marvin said, and he turned to scamper up the vine.

"I'm sure the king will be disappointed that you couldn't come," the royal messenger called after him.

But Marvin didn't hear him. He had already swung into his house and slammed the door behind him.

Meanwhile, back at the palace, King Leonard entered the grand ballroom and was very pleased to see that the preparations were nearly complete. A vast table, brightly decorated with flowers and colorful balloons, stood in the middle of the hall. Streamers and banners hung from the ceiling. Jesters practiced their juggling, and clowns in funny costumes adjusted their noses and baggy pants. In one corner, a musical band tuned up its instruments and made ready to play out a cheerful tune. The royal bakers scurried about with platters of scrumptious-looking cakes, cookies, doughnuts, and fine pastries.

Horatio greeted the king. "Good afternoon, Sire," the thin bird said with a salute. "The time has come to begin freezing the ice cream, and the royal dessert makers are ready to commence at your word."

A cluster of cooks stood motionless near the ice-cream-making equipment, breathlessly awaiting the king's signal.

"Gentlemen," King Leonard said, raising his paw high into the air, "let the ice cream begin!"

This sent the cooks into a frenzy of activity. One began stirring a huge pan full of syrupy cream, another began to shovel ice into a tall silver bowl, and others climbed up to a platform over the bowl and carefully measured out ingredients.

"You have done a fine job, Horatio," the king said, patting the thin bird on the back. "A fine job indeed!"

"I am glad you are pleased, Sire," Horatio beamed. "Oh, excuse me a moment. I see that the royal messengers have just arrived." With a flutter of his wings, he was at their sides in a corner of the ballroom.

As he listened to each messenger, Horatio could hardly believe his ears. With a frown on his face, the thin bird returned to the king.

"Well," the king asked, "are there any animals who will not be attending?"

"I'm afraid so, Sire," Horatio said quietly.

"Who might they be?" King Leonard inquired.

"Ah, they, they—" Horatio stuttered.

"Yes?" the king prodded.

"Henry Hyena—" the bird began.

"Oh, what a shame! He is such a jovial sort."

"—and Zelda the Zebra."

"Oh. She will be missed."

"And Marvin Monkey," Horatio continued.

"How terrible!" the king exclaimed, shaking his head. "He's such an energetic little fellow. But at least there are only three who cannot attend."

Horatio cleared his throat and hung his head.

"There aren't any others, are there?" the king asked.

"There are several other names," the thin bird confessed.

"How dreadful. Who are they?"

"Let me see," Horatio said, looking at his list. "Wally Water Buffalo, Sam the Snake and his sister Susie, Hubert Hippopotamus, Elizabeth the Elephant—"

"Oh, my," King Leonard moaned, putting his paw over his face. "What of my cat friends?"

Horatio grimaced. "Patricia Panther, Tom the Tiger, Charles the Cheetah—"

"And the apes?" the king asked hopefully.

"I mentioned Marvin Monkey," the bird began, "also Opra the Orangutan, Gregory Gorilla, Chuck the Chimp—"

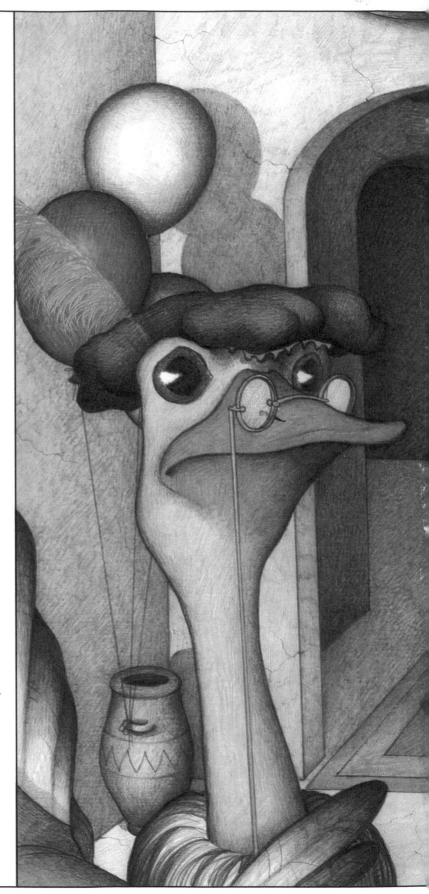

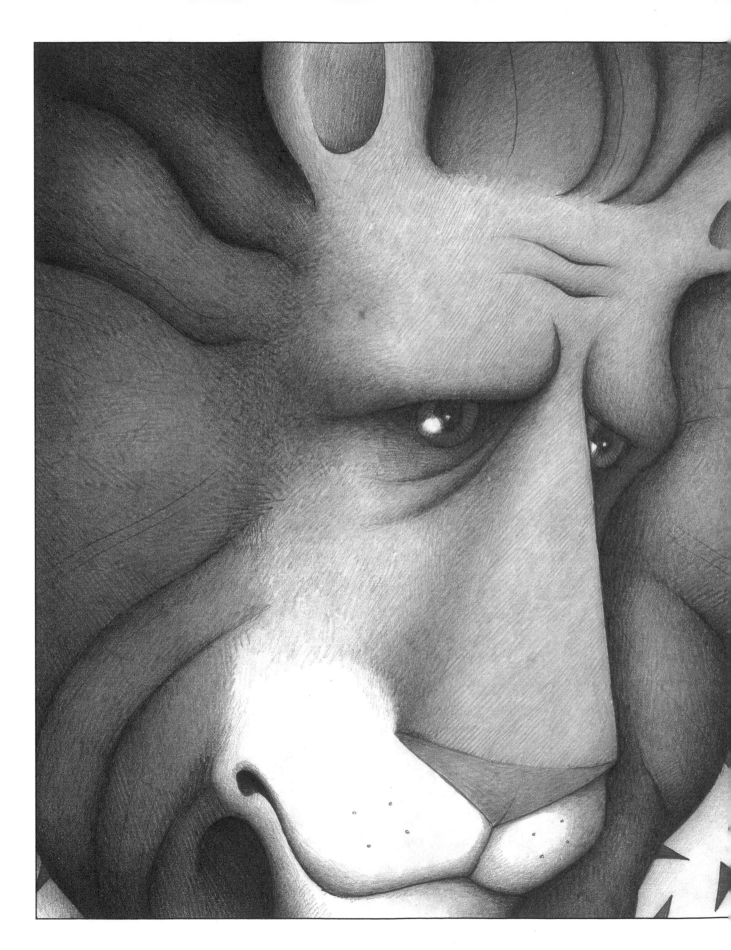

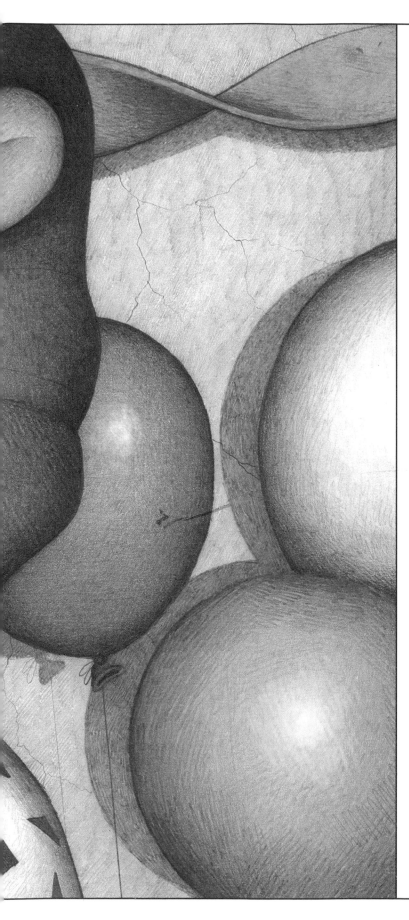

"None of them will be attending?" King Leonard asked, his face beginning to fill with disappointment.

Horatio just sighed and shook his head no.

"But why, Horatio?" the king asked quizzically.

Horatio shrugged his shoulders. "Apparently they are busy, Sire. One mentioned traveling. Another said she wanted to play with some new things she had gotten. Another—"

"Enough!" the king said, waving his paw. "Tell me, Horatio, who can come?"

The thin bird swallowed hard before answering. "No one, Sire," he quietly squawked.

"What was that?" the king asked. "Speak up."

"No one, Sire," Horatio repeated in little more than a whisper.

The king began to laugh. "It sounded as though you said 'no one,' " he chuckled.

"Yes, Sire," Horatio confessed, "I did. No one will be coming to your celebration."

Horatio had never seen King Leonard look so sad. "Not even one of my subjects will be coming?" he asked sorrowfully.

"I am very sorry, Sire," Horatio said, trying to comfort his king. "Would you like me to have the streamers taken down and the food put into the royal refrigerators?"

"I suppose so. . . . We don't want it to go to waste."

"And what shall I do with the ice cream, Sire?" Horatio asked. "The cooks have already begun making it."

"It must be disposed of, I suppose," the king lamented. "It certainly will not save."

"Yes, Sire," the thin bird said with a salute and a bow.

It was just then, as Horatio was about to order the cooks to discontinue their work on the ice cream and to order the other servants to begin taking down the festive decorations, that King Leonard had another idea. Just when the party seemed doomed to failure, he had a wonderful, brilliant idea.

"Wait, Horatio!" the king loudly ordered.

"Sire?" he answered, surprised by the lion's roar.

"Allow the cooks to continue with the royal ice cream!" he said forcefully.

"But, Sire, who will eat it?" Horatio asked.

King Leonard stroked his mane and thought out loud. "My subjects will not attend the celebration, eh? Then we shall have to carry on without them. Make up new invitations immediately, Horatio!" he shouted. "Send my messengers out and have them invite any and all animals they can find."

"But, Sire," Horatio objected, "the jungle animals said . . . "

"Yes, I know," the lion interrupted. "Have the messengers go to the towns outside the jungle."

"If I might make a suggestion, your Highness?" Horatio said timidly. "The animals outside the jungle are . . . well, they are not well groomed or colorful. They just aren't as polite as your own subjects."

"Polite?" the king roared. "My own animals have rudely declined my invitation. Now send forth the messengers! Tell them to be quick! I want this hall filled by the time the ice cream is ready!"

Horatio saluted, bowed, and went to carry out the king's command. "Royal messengers!" he squawked

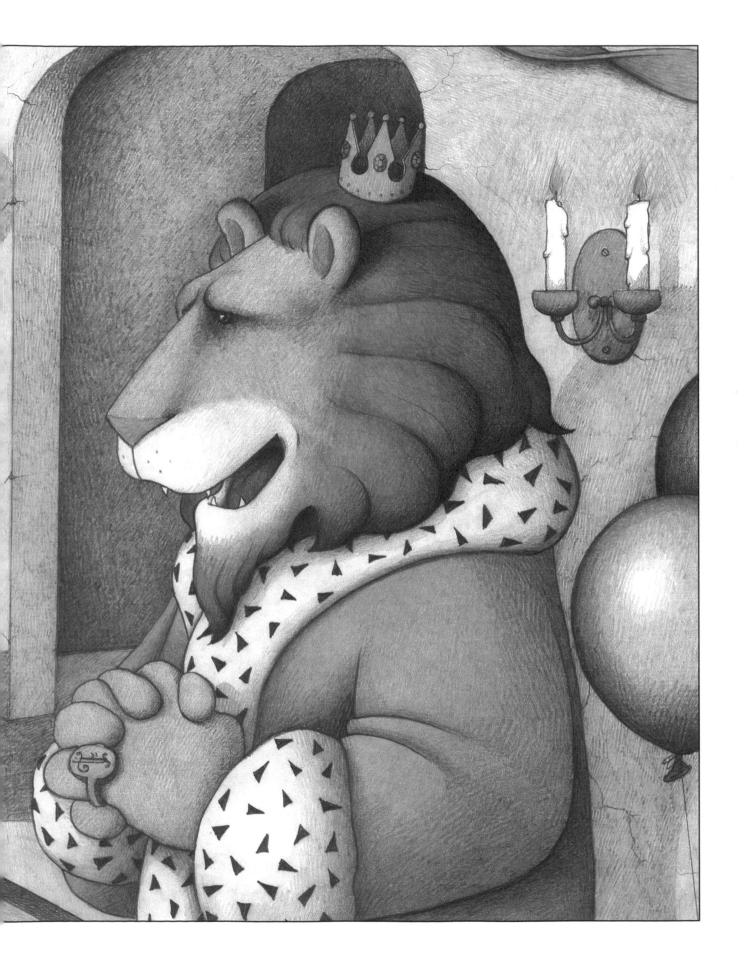

So again the king's fleet-footed messengers went to and fro delivering invitations to the royal celebration. This time they journeyed outside the jungle barrier to the great towns in the forests, and even as far as the cities by the sea. They handed out invitations for King Leonard's party to everyone they saw. There were raccoons, opossums, sea gulls, loons, and an assortment of moose. There were a pair of otters, several woodpeckers, and three young foxes. Invitations were given to some bears, a woodchuck, a couple eagles, and a porcupine or two. There were even several kangaroos and a grumpy old wallaby who were invited to the royal celebration.

Many of the animals were rather dirty and some had only rags for clothes, yet unlike the animals of the jungle, these humble creatures gladly agreed to come. They skipped about for joy when they heard the news. They felt honored that a great lion king had asked them to come to his home. Happily they followed the messengers to the king's palace, where they were given baths and clothed in beautiful garments.

Upon completing his task, Horatio hurried back to where the king was waiting in the throne room. "Sire, the—the messengers have carried out your request," the thin bird said between huffs and puffs.

"Yes?" King Leonard said, raising his furry eyebrows. "And have they returned with partygoers?"

"Yes, Sire," Horatio nodded proudly.

The king clapped his paws together loudly. "Very good! Well done, Horatio!"

"But, Sire," the bird hesitated, "there are still a few empty seats at the banquet table."

"Well, we can't have that! Is the ice cream ready yet?"

"Almost, Sire."

"Call for the messengers once again," the king commanded. "Send them . . . to . . . the country. Yes, the country it is. And tell them to be quick!"

"Yes, Sire," he said with a salute, and then disappeared in a flurry of feathers. "Royal messengers!" he squawked once again.

The messengers went out one last time. They went to the country, even as far as Pupland and Varmintsville, and invited all the animals they could find. There were horses, cows, roosters, and pigs of all sizes. There were hound dogs, barn cats, a gaggle of geese, and several sheep. There were even two stubborn mules and a pushy billy goat. News of the king's celebration made them all quite happy, and they immediately dropped what they were doing to follow the messengers back to the castle.

After the animals were assembled, King Leonard entered the banquet hall. He was delighted with what he saw. There, in the midst of the festive banners, colorful balloons, and decorations, were hundreds of smiling faces eagerly awaiting the start of the celebration.

Upon seeing the king, the guests gasped with surprise and wonder. They oohed and aahed at his beautiful golden mane as it flowed out over his shimmering purple robe. They pointed and marveled at the sparkling crown set firmly upon his royal head. He looked even more kingly than any of the animals had imagined. All at once the crowd grew quiet and bowed before him.

"Greetings, my new friends," King Leonard called out in a regal-sounding tone.

"Greetings, your Highness," they responded.

"I welcome you all," the king continued. "I am so glad that you could attend today. It is my hope that you will greatly enjoy this time of celebration!"

Stepping to his seat and lifting his punch-filled goblet high into the air, King Leonard roared his official pronouncement: "Let the party begin!"

To the animals' surprise, balloons suddenly dropped from the high ceiling, bright fireworks exploded, and a flock of colorful birds took flight. It was all quite delightful, and the crowd joined in, shouting cheers and blowing on the noisemakers, tooters, and horns that had been set next to their plates.

Above the roar of the crowd, King Leonard addressed the royal band. "Let there be music!"

The music and games began, and the ballroom was filled with happy sounds. Then Horatio spoke a word in the king's ear. The lion smiled and jumped up from his seat. "My dear guests," he said with a cublike smile on his face, "it is my pleasure to announce that the royal ice cream is now served!"

To this the crowd cheered.

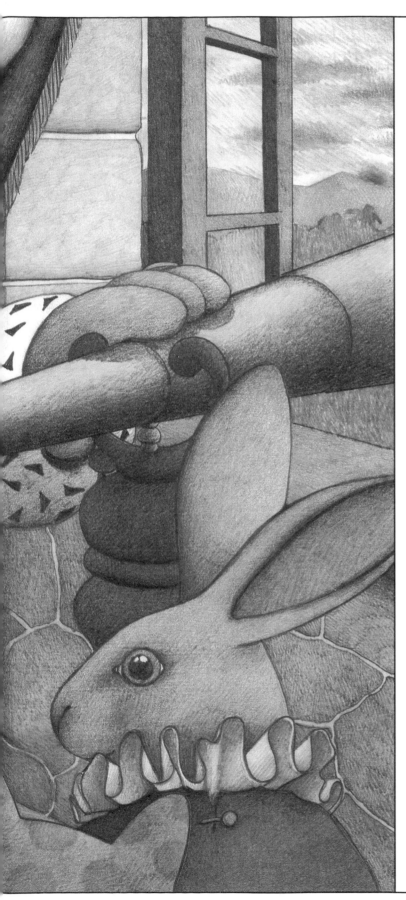

"After you have eaten as much as you desire," the king explained, "we will commence with more special games and songs!"

Again the animals cheered.

And so it was that King Leonard's celebration began. And what a celebration it was. How the king enjoyed being with his new friends. He talked with them, walked with them, shared in their games, and even let them look through his royal telescope.

The animal guests had a splendid time with the lion king. In fact, they enjoyed his company so much that when they were getting tired and the morning was dawning, they did not want to return to their own homes.

In the end, King Leonard invited them to stay and live with him in his palace. The animals were overwhelmed by the king's generosity and agreed with joy.

So the party was extended. Day after day, the king and his animal friends played, sang, and ate ice cream. Day after day, King Leonard's celebration continued.

The End

You can read a story like this in the Bible. Jesus told it in Luke 14:15–24:

When one of those at the table with him heard this, he said to Jesus, "Blessed is the man who will eat at the feast in the kingdom of God."

Jesus replied: "A certain man was preparing a great banquet and invited many guests. At the time of the banquet he sent his servant to tell those who had been invited, 'Come, for everything is now ready.'

"But they all alike began to make excuses. The first said, 'I have just bought a field, and I must go and see it. Please excuse me.'

"Another said, 'I have just bought five yoke of oxen, and I'm on my way to try them out. Please excuse me.'

"Still another said, 'I just got married, so I can't come.'

"The servant came back and reported this to his master. Then the owner of the house became angry and ordered his servant, 'Go out quickly into the streets and alleys of the town and bring in the poor, the crippled, the blind, and the lame.'

" 'Sir,' the servant said, 'what you ordered has been done, but there is still room.'

"Then the master told his servant, 'Go out to the roads and country lanes and make them come in, so that my house will be full. I tell you, not one of those men who were invited will get a taste of my banquet.' "